MASSACHUSETTS

PORTRAIT OF THE LAND AND ITS PEOPLE

VOLUME 2: TODAY

by Georgia Orcutt

American Geographic Publishing
Helena, Montana

William A. Cordingley, Chairman
Rick Graetz, Publisher
Mark Thompson, Director of Publications
Barbara Fifer, Production Manager

Library of Congress Cataloging-in-Publication Data

(Revised for vol. 2.)

Orcutt, Georgia.
    Massachusetts, portrait of the land and its people.
    (Massachusetts geographic series ; no. 1-   )
    Bibliography: p.
    Contents: v. 1. Yesterday—v. 2. Today
    1. Massachusetts--Historical geography. 2. Historic sites--Massachu-
setts--Guide-books. 3. Massachusetts--Description and travel.   I. Title.
F64.073 1988   974.4   88-22212
ISBN 0-938314-45-9 (v. 1)
ISBN 0-938314-42-4 (v. 2)

ISBN 0-938314-42-4

© 1988 American Geographic Publishing, P.O. Box 5630,
Helena, MT 59604. (406) 443-2842.

Text © 1988 Georgia Orcutt.

Design by Linda Collins.

Printed in Korea by Dong-A Printing Co.

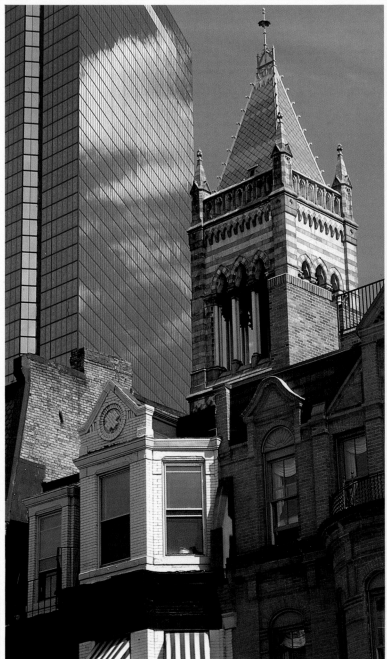

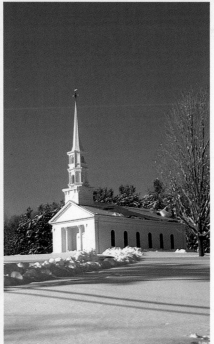

Front cover: *Boston Harbor.* CLYDE SMITH

Back cover: MIKE MAZZASCHI; STOCK BOSTON

Title page: BRUCE HANDS

Facing page, left: *Boats for work and play near Gloucester.* JAMES RANDKLEV

Right: *Newburyport.* ROBERT PERRON

This page, far left: *Homes of Boston's Back Bay, with the Hancock Tower beyond.* RICHARD PASLEY; STOCK BOSTON

Left: *The Martha-Mary Chapel, Sudbury.*

JOHN A. LYNCH

Above: *Shades of yesterday in Provincetown.*

FRANK S. BALTHIS

3

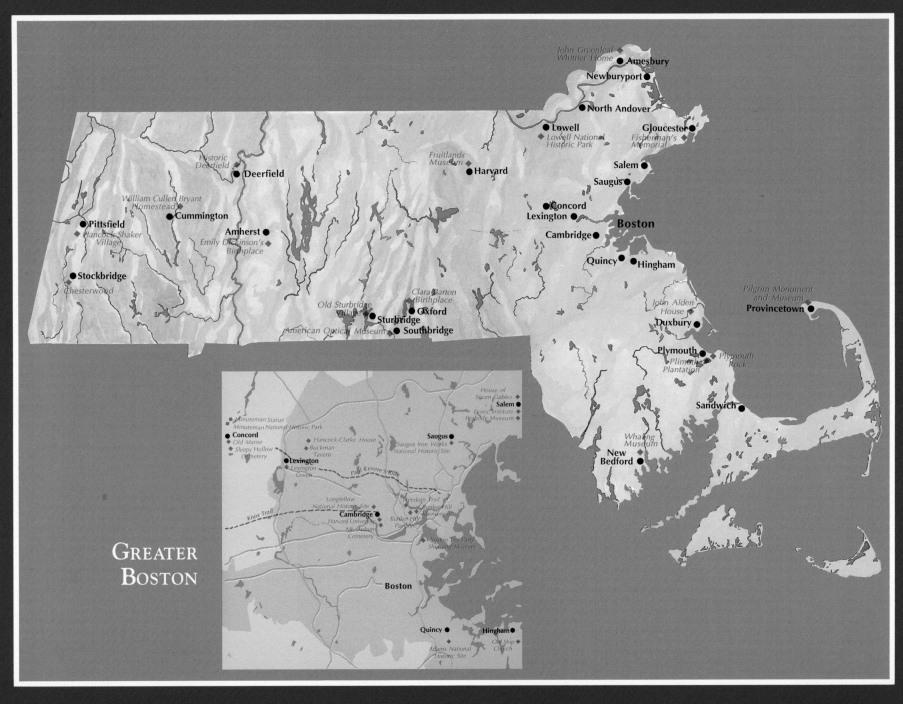

John Greenleaf
Whittier Home
● **Amesbury**

● **Newburyport**

● **North Andover**

● **Lowell**
◆ *Lowell National
Historic Park*

● **Gloucester**
◆ *Fisherman's
Memorial*

*Historic
Deerfield*
● **Deerfield**

*Fruitlands
Museum*
● **Harvard**

● **Salem**

● **Saugus**

*William Cullen Bryant
Homestead*
● **Cummington**

● **Pittsfield**
◆ *Hancock Shaker
Village*

● **Amherst**
*Emily Dickinson's
Birthplace*

● **Concord**
● **Lexington**

● **Boston**

● **Cambridge**

● **Stockbridge**
Chesterwood

*Clara Barton
Birthplace*

● **Quincy**
● **Hingham**

*Old Sturbridge
Village*
● **Sturbridge**

● **Oxford**

American Optical Museum
● **Southbridge**

*John Alden
House*

*Pilgrim Monument
and Museum*
◆ ● **Provincetown**

● **Duxbury**

● **Plymouth**
◆ *Plimoth
Plantation*
*Plymouth
Rock*

● **Sandwich**

*Whaling
Museum*
● **New
Bedford**

GREATER BOSTON

Minuteman Statue
◆ *Minuteman National Historic Park*

*House of
Seven Gables* ◆
● **Salem**
Essex Institute
Peabody Museum ◆

● **Concord**
◆ *Old Manse*
◆ *Sleepy Hollow
Cemetery*

Hancock-Clarke House
◆ *Buckman
Tavern*

*Saugus Iron Works
National Historic Site*
● **Saugus**

● **Lexington**
*Lexington
Green*

Paul Revere's Ride

*Longfellow
National Historic Site*
● **Cambridge**
Harvard University
*Mt. Auburn
Cemetery*

Knox Trail

Freedom Trail
*Bunker Hill
Monument*
*Bunker Hill
Pavilion*

*Boston Tea Party
Ship and Museum*

● **Boston**

● **Quincy**
*Adams National
Historic Site*

● **Hingham**
*Old Ship ◆
Church*

CONTENTS

MAP   4

INTRODUCTION   6

CHAPTER 1
THE PEOPLE   10

CHAPTER 2
THE LAND   36

CHAPTER 3
BOSTON   52

CHAPTER 4
THE STATE   70

FOR FURTHER READING   103

Lowell. FRANK SITEMAN; STOCK BOSTON

INTRODUCTION

Massachusetts, that place back East beside the ocean, has become a symbol of many things in the national imagination. With a repetitiveness that is striking, if a bit wearisome, American history textbooks have told the same story to well over a dozen generations of schoolchildren: first Columbus, then the early explorers, then Plymouth, then the founding of the bayside colony of Massachusetts. In his 1868 edition of *A Child's History of the United States,* John Bonner wrote: "As long as the world lasts, that Rock [Plymouth] will be known and honored as the spot where the Pilgrim fathers rested from their journey and set foot in the land where their children were destined to become a great and powerful nation."

Citizens of Massachusetts have rivaled the historians in extolling the virtues of their state. For the Puritans, Boston was to be a "citte on a hill" that would shine like a beacon to show the way to true Protestant Christian faith. For the publicists of the Revolutionary war, Massachusetts was a "cradle of liberty." In the heady days of the nineteenth century Boston was dubbed the "Hub of the Universe" while Massachusetts was called by many the nation's "Republic of Letters."

While history and literature have ensured Massachusetts an important place in the imagination of out-of-staters, more recent events have kept the Commonwealth in the limelight. The presidential election of 1972 reinforced the image of Massachusetts as a progressive, if at times off-beat, state. In that year Massachusetts had the distinction of being the only state to support George McGovern, and for the next

Left: Acoxet.
Facing page: *On Walden Pond.* CLYDE H. SMITH PHOTOS

four years many residents proudly sported buttons and bumper stickers saying: "Don't Blame Me. I'm From Massachusetts."

Massachusetts governor Michael Dukakis, a son of the state's Greek community, has become a national figure in a very short time. Known for combining sound fiscal management and a conciliatory approach to Massachusetts business interests, he also shows a sensitivity to the human needs of many citizens who continue to live on the fringe of the current economic boom. In the course of the current presidential nomination campaign, one hears a great deal about the "Massachusetts Miracle." In the past two decades or so, a new sense of prosperity and future possibility *has* been in the air. For those living in Massachusetts, the change has been conspicuous. Dukakis is a leader who has attempted to guarantee economic well being to all Bay State residents. Under his guidance Massachusetts is moving toward a plan that will provide universal health insurance to all its citizens.

Those who are culturally rather than politically inclined will have other immediate associations with Massachusetts. They might think first of Boston's outstanding collection of Asian art in the Museum of Fine Arts, a legacy of the days when the black sheep from Boston's brahmin families pioneered America's interest in Hindu religion and Zen Buddhism. Cognoscenti in the theater recall the old Provincetown Players on Cape Cod, trail blazers in the collectivist theater movement of the early twentieth century, founded by such Greenwich Village luminaries as Hapgood Hutchins, Eugene O'Neill and Mable Dodge. Aficionados of classical music are certainly impressed by the world-class reputation of the Boston Symphony Orchestra, and its beloved summer home, Tanglewood, in the Berkshires. Late great conductor of the Boston Pops, Arthur Fiedler, son of the local German Jewish community, led that organization to national and world-wide fame for its entertaining, well-performed

music and concerts on the banks of the Charles.

The Charles River itself sets memories in motion for an entirely different set of Americans who remember Massachusetts for the 1960s rock song praising Boston's dirty water. For a slightly older generation, Boston might mean another popular song which immortalized the story of poor Charley who, for want of a dime, was for all time trapped on the Boston subway.

Many a couple who courted in the late 1940s and early 1950s would certainly recall with nostalgia the sentimental refrain from the then-popular tune about Cape Cod.

The more serious and competitive would certainly think of higher education. The Boston area alone has scores of colleges and universities aside from Harvard, once a provincial Puritan divinity school but now a world class university, or M.I.T., an institution renowned for its pioneering studies in bio-medical research, computers and physics. The entrepreneurial sort would certainly site the Bay State's booming computer industry, a phenomenon that has catapulted Massachusetts—along with Japan and California's Silicon Valley—to high tech fame.

For Pentagon and military buffs the Commonwealth could just as well mean lucrative contracts for sophisticated weapons and cutting edge defense contracts. And in a distinctly different vein, Massachusetts certainly means for many others extraordinary medical care and health research carried on at both the major local universities and at hospitals.

Sports fans always have something to say—good or bad about the Boston teams. The Red Sox are known for their sentimental Fenway Park and the mistake they can't overcome. (In 1918, after winning several World Series, they traded their star pitcher, Babe Ruth, to the New York Yankees; with the Yankees Ruth became the greatest home run hitter in baseball history. And every time the Red Sox have made it into the Series since, they have lost at the seventh game.) The Boston Bruins spawned Bobby Orr, the first defenseman to score 100 points in one season; his prowess changed the way defensemen would play hockey. The Celtics, who play in Boston Garden, the last of the old-time arenas, have proved to be the most successful franchise in professional sports history. They have won 16 world championships since 1957—eight in a row.

Certainly millions of people know of the Boston Marathon, once the oldest amateur road race in the country, now one of the increasingly lucrative spectacles that offers runners an attractive piece of the celebrity pie.

For others the most powerful images are sea and quietude—the rocky harbors and coves of the North and South shores, the dunes, beaches and surf of the Cape, tinged perhaps with the nostalgia and national tragedies associated with the Kennedy Compound at Hyannis. For many, Boston and Massachusetts must mean, above all else, the Kennedys. In May of 1989, a statue of JFK in mid-stride will be unveiled on the Statehouse lawn. The 28-member commission in charge of the memorial has yet to resolve whether the former President's top suit coat button should be buttoned, as it is in virtually every picture of him, or left open, as most of them would like to remember him.

Right: *Waves near Gloucester.* CLYDE H. SMITH
Facing page: *Boston.* FRANK S. BALTHIS

THE PEOPLE

Over the course of its 350-year history, Massachusetts has spawned an impressive and lengthy list of leaders who continue to influence the entire nation (not to mention the world) in almost every field, especially the arts, science, technology and politics.

The state's climate has always encouraged independent thinking. Ironically, this intellectual freedom can trace its roots to the 17th-century Puritans, who favored conformity but demanded literate congregations who could read the Bible and discuss it. In 1636, the Massachusetts General Court established a college to educate Puritan clergy; John Harvard donated his money, his books and his name, ensuring that "the light of learning might not go out..." During the 19th century that light burned brightly and before 1900 a formidable group of private colleges had been founded in Massachusetts: Williams; Amherst; Wheaton; Holy Cross; Tufts; Boston College; Massachusetts Institute of Technology; Boston University; Wellesley; Smith; Radcliffe; Mount Holyoke; Clark; Northeastern; and Simmons.

The list of writers who found their voices in the 19th century—and whose work still occupies a prominent place in textbooks, includes the giants of American literature: Ralph Waldo Emerson, Nathaniel Hawthorne, the Alcotts, Henry David Thoreau, John Greenleaf Whittier, Herman Melville, Oliver Wendell Holmes, Henry Wadsworth Longfellow, Emily Dickinson. Holmes and James Russell Lowell worked together on *The Atlantic Monthly* in Boston, which continues a tradition of publishing excellent fiction and

Left: *The Longfellow home in Cambridge.* JIM CRONK
Facing page: *Harvard University.* CLYDE H. SMITH

features. An impressive list of contemporary writers including John Updike, James Carroll, Anne Bernays and Doris Kearns call Massachusetts home today.

The first of Massachusetts' acclaimed artists painted the American gentry. John Singleton Copley, born of Irish parents in Boston in 1737, established himself as a successful painter of portraits; a number of his paintings mirroring the life of Boston's aristocracy, plus likenesses of Revolutionary heroes Samuel Adams, John Quincy Adams and Joseph Warren hang in Boston's Museum of Fine Arts. James Abbott McNeill Whistler, born in Lowell in 1834, developed a haunting impressionist style and used it to create a world-famous tribute to his mother. Winslow Homer, born in Boston in 1836, developed a fresh original style of watercolors in Gloucester and began a new school of American genre paintings. Decades later, Edward Hopper saw scenes to paint along Gloucester's seacoast before discovering the perfect light and solitude on Cape Cod.

Concord's Daniel Chester French decided to try his hand at sculpture and became world famous for his efforts, which include the Minuteman Statue unveiled in 1875 at Concord's Centennial Celebration, and the Seated Lincoln in Washington. Gilbert Stuart, a Rhode Islander by birth, set up his studio in Boston and made it his business to paint the presidents; his portraits of George and Martha Washington have become national treasures. Starting in the late 19th century and continuing into the 1940s various schools of artists and their students sought out the solitude and beauty of quiet Massachusetts seacoast villages such as Gloucester, Rockport and Provincetown.

Massachusetts also inspired early leaders in the labor movement. The importance given to thrift and hard work among the Puritans on the frontier in the 17th century was transformed by the industrial revolution of the 19th century into a difficult and exhausting way of life for many of the state's residents. Puritan Edward Johnson, in his 1654 tribute to the Bay Colony—A

Wonder-Working Providence—marveled at the way in which settlers "caused their little ones to be very diligent in spinning cotton wool." Johnson was referring to the "putting-out system," the standard, family-based means of organizing Massachusetts textile production until the rise of more centralized and mechanized industry. Under the new mill regime of the 19th century however, the question of labor—for children, for women, and even for men—became a struggle central to the life of the nation.

The first union-style organization was founded in early 1823. By the 1830s mill workers had begun to ask for rights, many of which today we take for granted: free public education, the abolition of monopolies, the end of imprisonment for debt, the separation of religion from politics. In the 19th and early 20th centuries, through the financial panics of 1837, 1857, 1893 and 1907, in the depressions of the 1870s, 1884 and 1921, and during the great crisis of 1929 and since, many Massachusetts men and women struggled to improve the lot of working people. Most remain anonymous, or are remembered only in factory records, union journals and ship's logs, but their efforts helped to create the American way of life we so highly value today. A few of the many Massachusetts labor pioneers included George McNeil, a weaver from Fall River, Ira Steward, a machinist from Boston who was one of the first to advocate an eight-hour work day, and a host of influential women from the textile mills such as Sarah Bagley and Lucy Larcom, a poet and author of the famous *A New England Girlhood*.

Massachusetts was a pioneer in child labor laws. In 1842 it became law that children under 12 limit their

Right: *An old life-saving station at Race Point Beach on Cape Cod National Seashore.*
Facing page: *Captain John Parker of the Lexington Militia, honored by this statue on the site, was felled by a British musket on April 19, 1775.* JEFF GNASS PHOTOS

work in the mill to 10 hours per day, and in 1858 employed children were required to have 18 weeks of schooling per year. The first enforceable law for children's eight-hour work days was passed in 1913. As recently as 1937 it became illegal for minors under 14 to work during school hours; no children under 16 could sell papers or "exercise the trade of scavenger."

The Massachusetts labor movement also made its mark on commercial shipping and fisheries, influencing a number of historic strikes, such as the one that began on July 4, 1918 when 5,000 New England fishermen struck for 38 days. Shipboard conditions could be extremely hard. A sailor risked his life and worked in constant danger for very little pay, enduring harsh discipline and crowded ships. Whaling ships, known as "floating factories," required the skills of mechanics, artisans, coopers and smiths just to sustain life at sea on the year-long voyages. Sailors learned early that what was called a strike on land was mutiny at sea, and they often found themselves in irons. Like the much maligned company store, most of a seaman's wages for a voyage might end up charged against the ship's books; the remainder was likely to be spent in sailor's boarding houses during the few weeks on shore. The only item that was dispensed free to all New Bedford sailors was the King James Bible, what one fleet owner called "a ship owner's best and cheapest investment."

The most famous and protracted strikes occurred in the shoe and textile industries that formed the backbone of the Massachusetts economy during most of the 19th century. With the failure of the Utopian schemes of the early visionary mill owners (the cities of Lowell and Lawrence, for example), the laboring public

Left: A chilly day at Thoreau's Walden Pond near Concord. GEORGE WUERTHNER

Facing page: Fishing boats in the Provincetown harbor on Cape Cod. JEFF GNASS

found itself at the mercy of centralized industry. The first important strike in Massachusetts occurred in 1858-1859 in Natick, when , after a protracted 14-week struggle, 600 shoe workers gained a modest increase in wages. A year later the labor movement spread like wildfire when 1,000 shoemakers formed a union and called a strike in Lynn. Lynn's mayor appointed 100 special police and called in 100 additional Boston patrolmen. In the following week, the strike generally spread throughout eastern Massachusetts, and was joined by women stitchers, binders and machine operators. Workers from Marblehead, Danvers, Salem, Beverly and Woburn joined the Lynn workers in March, 1860, for what was the largest labor demonstration to date in Massachusetts. Five thousand men and 1,000 women workers carried hundreds of banners and 26 American flags through the streets of Lynn, accompanied by military and fire companies and five brass bands. Although the strike was broken with scab labor imported from Maine and New Hampshire, the labor movement was established as a fact of life in Massachusetts.

Much of the Massachusetts abolitionist spirit carried on into the union campaigns of the late 19th century. Prominent middle class reformers such as Wendell Phillips, Josiah Warren, William Channing, Albert Brisbane and John Orvis participated in, or at least supported, the aspiration of trade unionism. One political offshoot of the labor movement—the Independent Party, formed in 1870—succeeded in electing 21 state representatives and one state senator in an overnight campaign. Yet gains were made slowly. By 1879 there were 42 trade unions in the state.

Left: *Visitor center at Lowell Industrial Park, which tells the story of the cloth-milling industry.* FREDRIK D. BODIN; STOCK BOSTON
Facing page: *Concord River in Lowell Industrial Park.*
MARY ANN BROCKMAN

Between 1881 and 1900 there were more than 1800 recorded strikes and lockouts. Despite its small size, Massachusetts during these years was fourth among all states in strikes, and third in the number of lockouts.

In 1911, the hours a woman could work in a mill were reduced by legislation to 54 per week. When, in retaliation, manufacturers reduced wages proportionally, the complaints of laborers and their supporters precipitated one of the most famous labor struggles of Massachusetts history: the Great Lawrence Strike of 1912. (At the time of this great event, the average Massachusetts male factory worker took home approximately $8.76 per week—after the company "store" took its bite.) Although the workers were only loosely organized, the management move galvanized the laborers. After three days nearly all semi-skilled and unskilled laborers were out. When the leadership of the strike was taken over by the I.W.W. (Industrial Workers of the World), mass picket lines went up throughout Lawrence. In response, the mayor requisitioned four out-of-town militia troops to join the city's four local troops. When the president of the American Woolen Company refused to meet with labor, skilled operatives joined the strike. Dynamite was discovered and seven strikers were arrested and charged, despite the fact that evidence pointed to agents of management. As local friction increased, four more companies of militia were called in.

During a huge demonstration on January 29, a woman striker was killed. At this point the city council voted to turn the town over to militia control. Ten more companies of infantry and two of cavalry joined the fray. The strikers' children were sent out of town for

---

Left: *Fishermen at work on Cape Cod.* CLYDE H. SMITH
Facing page: *A typical narrow street in Marblehead.* BRUCE HANDS

protection, but as one group of what were called "refugee children" attempted to board a train, the militia moved in, clubbing parents and children alike; whole families were arrested and taken off to jail.

In response to this incident, the largest picket line in Massachusetts history was raised with more than 20,000 workers. In time the strikers won; their concession included wage increases, time-and-a-quarter for overtime, and guarantees of non-discrimination against union members. Although the Lawrence strike was a spectacular event and its gains for workers were significant, tension between labor and management continued for decades.

Women played a crucial role in Massachusetts labor history. (Of the 122,389 textile workers in Massachusetts in 1937, 40 percent were women.) Most women workers entered the mills at a very early age and remained there for the greater part of their lives. Even marriage rarely took them away from their jobs, since their husbands' salaries seldom sufficed to support a family. While wages rose, so did productivity demands: a wage increase of 10 percent was accompanied by a workload increase of 25 to 200 percent. In 1921, Florence Luscomb, an organizer for the International Ladies Garment Workers Union and a suffrage activist, drew attention to the deplorable conditions in the Boston sweatshops, precipitating yet another strike. Other industries joined the cause. In April 1919 Julie O'Connor led the Boston Telephone Operators out on strike with the support of the International Brotherhood of Electrical Workers. When phone service was tied up throughout the state, management

Left: *The windmill of Eastham is the oldest of Cape Cod mills.*
JEFF GNASS
Facing page: *Snow-plowing, traditional-style, in Concord.*
CLYDE H. SMITH

capitulated to workers' demands and wages increased from $16 to $19 a week.

Another noteworthy moment in Massachusetts labor history occurred in 1919 when more than 1200 Boston policemen voted to join the American Federation of Labor. When the Police Commissioner ordered them to desist from their organizing efforts, the Policemen's Union went out on strike. Then, as now, a strike mounted by a police force is a highly controversial and dangerous affair, so many of Boston's major institutions were drawn into the battle. President Lowell of Harvard University appealed to the college men to prepare themselves for service to the city. One of the Harvard coaches was reported to have said: "To hell with football if men are needed." Sympathy for the police came from many Boston citizens who turned out to demonstrate against the 30 of a total of 420 patrolmen who did not go out on strike. When guardsmen opened fire on the crowd in South Boston, two boys were killed and several bystanders were wounded. Across town, a woman was killed during a calvary charge in Scollay Square. When rioting and looting broke out in the city, the strike became a national affair. President Wilson finally denounced the strike, as did Samuel Gompers of the American Federation of Labor. Eventually Governor Calvin Coolidge managed to break the strike, a move that catapulted him to national prominence and paved his path to the White House.

An increasing number of strikes encouraged manufacturers to pull their plants out of Massachusetts, and relocate first to New Hampshire, Maine and Canada, then later to the South. The readiness and frequency with which the shoe and textile plants were moved by their owners from Massachusetts to non-union states earned them the title of "factories on wheels." The effort on the part of labor continued throughout the 1930s and 1940s until wartime manpower needs both reduced the available work force, thereby strengthening the hand of the employees, and

accelerated the need for finished goods. After the war, with the older industries gone, the state faced several decades of decline that was overcome with the advent of the High Technology boom of the 1970s.

Although for two centuries Yankee elites dominated Massachusetts politics and economy, it was here that many of the great debates were won and lost over the issue of minority rights. With the opening of the factories in the 19th century, Massachusetts became a magnet for immigrants from northern and western Europe. They were needed as a source of inexpensive labor, and resisted any outsiders in a tightly-knit social community. In 1894, the Immigration Restriction League of Boston was founded by leading members of old Boston brahmin families such as the Lees, the Paines, the Saltonstalls and the Warrens. The distinguished Henry Cabot Lodge voiced commonly held sentiments when he supported the exclusion of what he thought of as the "alien races." The Immigration Restriction League was influential in closing what had been America's open door when, in 1924, Congress passed the National Origins Quota Act which limited European migration to 150,000 a year and, more importantly, set up quotas based on the number of immigrants already in the country. This, in effect, allocated most places in the new immigrant quota system to Great Britain, Ireland, Germany and Scandinavia.

Today, it is impossible to think about Massachusetts without considering its numerous and powerful immigrant communities. And above all else, when one thinks of Boston, one has to think of the Irish. Mike

Left: A lobsterman greets the dawn in Nantucket Harbor.
CLYDE H. SMITH
Facing page: *Cape Cod sunset.* FRANK S. BALTHIS

Barnicle, one of the city's current political pundits, has quipped in the *Boston Globe* that political basic training in Massachusetts has always meant "war games against WASPS." He sees life for the politically ambitious Democrats and Irish of Massachusetts as a kind of preset rite of passage: "You're born. You get baptized. You receive your first Holy Communion. You get confirmed. You run against a WASP. You win. And then you die. It's a part of life."

The people of Massachusetts will often joke about the close connections among religion, politics and ethnicity in the state's history, but today's humor is often a luxury that winners can afford once they've arrived. Like the rest of the nation, Massachusetts has undergone many demographic changes in the course of its history. But since it has been around longer than most other states, in the world of heartbreaks, struggles and victories that come with racial and religious diversity, Massachusetts was there first.

As late as 1850 an Irishman could not become a Boston policeman, even though one third of the city's population was Irish. The Irish had no political influence and no access to city jobs. Old families dating back to the colonial days and wealthy Anglo-Saxon arrivistes controlled the city and the state. However, by the 1850s, progressive brahmin Democrats came to depend upon the wealthy and conservative Irish to forge political coalitions. In 1895, Josiah Quincy, the last of the brahmin Democrats to be elected mayor, won his race with the support of the Irish ward bosses.

Family and neighborhood loyalties, old world prejudices and experiences, and the long struggle for

Left: *Viewing the concord River from Old North Bridge.* JIM CRONK
Facing page: *In the R.C. Nickerson State Forest Park on Cape Cod Peninsula.* JAMES RANDKLEV

James Michael Curley

That Boston's power has been shunted from Brahmin hands to the Irish was emphatically demonstrated by the ascendency in 1914 of James Michael Curley, a child of the Irish ghetto. Although he was opposed by Fitzgerald, he drew strong support from the Irish working class, prefering to leap over the Yankees and the old system of ward bosses. Curley was flamboyant, ambitious and egotistical, prone to fiery speeches and humorous denunciations of wealthy Brahmins and deeply aware of the experience of being Irish working class in Boston. The Irish loved him. Once he became mayor, he bought a mansion in Jamaica Plain (the fate of his house has recently become a preservation issue in Boston)—no Beacon Hill for him! He dismissed the old patronage employees and set in place his own, cutting ward bosses out of the action. They united against him, but Curley's political career continued. Although he was defeated as mayor in 1918, he was elected again in 1921. In 1924, when a provision limited the successive terms a mayor could serve, Curley ran for governor, and lost. In 1929 he ran again for mayor and won. His close association with Roosevelt propelled him into the governorship from 1934 to 1936. Beaten for the U.S. Senate by Henry Cabot Lodge Jr. and losing a bid for Boston mayor in 1937, he won a fourth term as mayor in 1945. His days of winning elections by bating Brahmins finally came to an end. He ran unsuccessfully for mayor in 1951 and 1955, and died in 1958.

equality in Boston and Massachusetts were the cement that eventually held together the emergence of local Irish political power. Beloved characters and their colorful stories have formed undying legends. In the 1880s there was "Smiling" Jim Donovan, a sharp dresser who wooed the Irish in the South End in Boston, Joe O'Connell who dominated Ward 20 in Dorchester, Pat Kennedy, the leader of East Boston, and most powerful of all, Martin Lomasney, who ran Ward 8 in the West End for more than 50 years.

In 1902 Patrick Collins was elected mayor, and the Irish Catholics triumphed again in 1905 with his re-election. His sudden death that same year cleared the way for John F. Fitzgerald ("Honey Fitz"), the ward boss of the North End, and the first American-born Irish to be elected mayor of Boston. Although the old guard Brahmins lined up against Fitzgerald by supporting James Jackson Storrow, Honey Fitz's re-election in 1910 marked a turning point in Massachusetts history: the emergence of a new style of politics, a phenomenon that resulted in the election of the first (and to the present day only) Catholic to the presidency of the United States. Politics became a route of upward mobility for the Irish, as it remains for many minority people today whose roots are well planted in Massachusetts.

The oldest black church building in America is in Boston and 10 sites forming the city's Black Heritage Trail point out important 18th- and 19th-century landmarks in black history. Among them is a memorial on Boston Common sculpted by Augustus Saint-Gaudens commemorating the first black regiment recruited during the Civil War.

Left: Faneuil Hall, Boston. JIM CRONK
Facing page: *The George Washington monument on Boston Common.* JEFF GNASS

Boston's large Black community dates from the 1890s when those disillusioned with Reconstruction and Jim Crow racism in the South headed to what many thought of as a promised land in the North. In Boston, they first settled in the old West End, then moved up the back of Beacon Hill to the South End, and by the 1920s moved into lower Roxbury. However, Boston was not the hospitable place they hoped to find. The newly powerful Irish were unsympathetic and unwilling to share any of the advances they had struggled for. Blacks were forced into low paying work and systematically excluded from the trades. Many worked at semi-skilled labor in the railroad yards and carved out a niche for themselves in the railroad service industries.

Black protest at the turn of the century was led by William Monroe Trotter, editor of *The Guardian*, an influential equal rights publication. His was not a conciliatory approach to the question of race. Rather, he addressed the fact that lynchings, the color line and the separate-but-equal idea were all indications that a caste system was developing in Massachusetts—and in the nation. On Patriot's Day, April 19, 1915, Trotter led a spirited company of 2,000 blacks up Beacon Street to the Statehouse toprotest the opening of D.W. Griffith's movie, *The Birth of a Nation*, with its blatant suggestions of white supremacy. When Governor David Walsh, Major Curley and the Police Commissioner Stephen O'Meara did not respond, violence broke out in the Tremont Theater. The episode galvanized moderate blacks of the NAACP and militants, two factions that had formerly been unable to resolve their differences.

Left: *Springtime on Newbury Street, Back Bay, Boston.*
MIKE MAZZASCHI; STOCK BOSTON
Facing page: *The mixture of old and new that characterizes Boston.* CLYDE H. SMITH

During the dark decade of 1970s bussing, it became painfully evident to the nation that racial tension was a major issue in the city. Anthony Lukas' book, *Common Ground*, tells the story of families caught up in the struggle and offers some fine insights into the conflicts that still trouble the city and the state.

The major Jewish immigration to Massachusetts began in the 1880s when pogroms in Russia and Central Europe forced Jews to uproot themselves and find a new life in a new land. Like other immigrant groups, they first settled in the older residential neighborhoods like the North and West ends of Boston. When arriving, many Jews opened shops or became itinerant peddlers. In the course of several decades, the more successful merchants formed an elite in the Jewish community and became major retailers in the Boston metropolitan area by the middle of the 20th century. As early as 1910 most Jews had left for North End for better neighborhoods in the western part of the city, such as Brookline. They also moved into several suburbs, such as Sharon, that now are centers for the Boston Jewish community.

The North End of Boston has long been known as the hub of Massachusetts' Italian community, home of wonderful pasta, pastries, pizza and the site of many festas and holidays celebrating the religious traditions of the old country. The North End was once a residential area of old colonial Boston, the only remnant of which is Paul Revere's home. By the early 19th century most of the oldest families had fled to the more spacious climes of Beacon Hill or Roxbury Heights, while recent immigrants began to flood in. First came the Irish, beginning in the early 19th century; later in the century

Left: *Naumkeag in Stockbridge.* MARY ANN BROCKMAN
Facing page: *The Ben Franklin statue at old city hall, Boston.* JIM CRONK

The Trying Times of Sacco and Vanzetti

In the midst of the decades of labor unrest, one of the most controversial events in all of Massachusetts history took place: the Sacco and Vanzetti Affair of 1920. Bartolomeo Vanzetti, a fish peddler, and Nicola Sacco, a shoe worker, both members of the Galleani group of anarchists, were arrested on the charge of murder and robbery in connection with the theft of a $15,000 payroll. Despite circumstantial evidence, alibis and commendations from former employers, they were found guilty. Their plight—which crystalized into that of workers vs. a powerful system—generated world-wide protests. Prominent Bostonians were called in to review the facts; President Lowell of Harvard, President Stratton of M.I.T. and others gave their opinion that Sacco and Vanzetti were guilty. Seven years after their arrests they were executed, triggering more protests and demonstrations. Today, scholars and historians agree that the whole incident was very much a political move caused by fear of radicals and workers, exacerbated by the fear of foreigners. The case remains open.

the Jews became the dominant group. While for outsiders the North End next became Little Italy, for insiders it represented a mosaic of old world allegiances, customs and cultures, the particularities of which defied the outsider's gaze. Traditions of the extended family and the village which were of determinative importance in Italy were transferred to Boston's North End. Like some Irish immigrants who retained a loyalty to Cork County or the Jews to their particular Polish or Rumanian villages, the early Italian immigrations lived in tightly-knit social units based upon the old country ways. As growth and development continue to transform the inner city, the future of Little Italy is uncertain.

The Chinese were the earliest Asians to settle in Massachusetts. They first came in the years after the Civil War when, having completed the first trans-continental railway, employers brought them east to act as strike-breakers during labor conflicts in the western part of the state. Like many other early immigrants, this was primarily a bachelor community made of young men who had left wives and families at home. Some drifted to Boston to form the nucleus of today's Chinatown community. In 1876, records indicate that Chinese were employed in the construction of Boston's Pearl Street Telegraph Exchange, on the site of what is now Chinatown.

As anti-Chinese sentiments grew on the west coast in the late 19th century, many more Chinese moved East. Following the Chinese Exclusion Act of 1882, more Chinese came to the Commonweaith as illegal aliens, traveling from the west coast of Canada to the

Left: *Boston experiences one of the pleasures of a four-season climate.*
Facing page: *Nighttime in Nantucket Harbor.*
CLYDE H. SMITH PHOTOS

East, where entry was easily gained to the New England states. The anti-Chinese bias in American immigration laws abated during World War II when China was a U.S. ally. As with so many other minorities, the local Chinese community was affected by the War Brides Act which allowed servicemen to bring their wives to the country. A real stimulus to Chinese immigration to Boston came about as a result of the civil rights movement of the 1960s, when the restrictive immigration quota system was finally changed due to its explicit racism. Boston's Chinatown began to grow rapidly, as families that had been separated for generations were reunited in the city.

The Chinese community today is made up of two distinct populations, one a Mandarin-speaking group whose origins are in Taiwan, and the other a Cantonese-speaking community from mainland China. Prosperous Chinese communities can be found today in Lexington, Quincy and Fall River. Chinatown is a vibrant part of Boston's downtown, hemmed in by development on many sides, but playing a large and influential role in development of New Boston.

The origins of a substantial Japanese community in Massachusetts rest in the dismal treatment of Japanese-Americans during World War II. After being interred in camps during the war years, many Japanese were discouraged from resettling in California. As part of a national dispersal program which sought to eliminate significant concentrations of Asians, a number of Japanese migrated to Massachusetts. A similar decentralization program has brought to Massachusetts a small Vietnamese community, now concentrated in Boston, Lawrence and Lowell.

The ethnic diversity recorded in the 1980 Massachusetts census reflects the complex history of the state. Of the almost 6 million people who live here, more than 5 million are listed as white, but the ancestry of this group reflects the successive waves of immigration to the state: 670,000 Irish, 450,000

English; 430,000 Italians; 312,000 French; 190,000 Portuguese; 160,000 Polish; 140,000 Hispanics. More than 225,000 Massachusetts residents are black, representing not only old-line Blacks who have been in the Commonwealth for a century and new transplants from the South, but Dominicans, Cubans and Haitians. The largest Asian population is the Chinese, who number 25,000, but Asian Indians, Koreans, Japanese and Filipinos, along with the recent influx of 3,000 Vietnamese, bring the total number of Asians to over 50,000.

Right: *Touring Quincy Market, Boston.*
JOHN COLETTE; STOCK BOSTON
Facing page: *Is Boston one of the most fitting settings for Old Glory?* FRANK S. BALTHIS

CHAPTER 2

THE LAND

The landscape of Massachusetts is beloved to many who have never seen it, but who have read Henry David Thoreau, the famous poet, diarist and hermit. His *Walden Pond* and *A Week on the Concord and Merrimack Rivers* virtually invented nature philosophy as a literary genre in the United States. Thoreau's words still captivate us today, and reading his books remains an excellent way to spend an afternoon in a rented canoe on the Merrimack or Concord rivers.

Massachusetts has changed a great deal in the last 150 years, however, and in May 1988, canoeist Denny Alsop paddled his canoe around Thoreau's Walden Pond to make a different kind of statement about nature: that we all must clean up and preserve our water. Alsop, a 41-year-old forester, was completing a 33-day-trip across Massachusetts by canoe with a cellular phone aboard, to remind the world that old technologies must be updated.

Land has always played a determinative role in the history of the Commonwealth. The early settlers were highly dependent on the natural abundance of wildlife; the first Thanksgiving was, after all, a common tribute by European pilgrims and native Americans to the bounty that could be reaped from Massachusetts fields, coasts, streams and forests.

The great fishing banks off the coast of Massachusetts drew Portuguese fishermen from the old country to the New World decades before the earliest English settlements began. The codfish in particular has been of tremendous importance to the Commonwealth, a fact symbolized by the effigy of a codfish that has hung in the State House on Beacon Hill since 1784.

Left: Scituate. CLYDE H. SMITH
Facing page: Walden Pond offers beauty still, but the solitude is gone. DAVID C. BINDER; STOCK BOSTON

The beaver and other fur-bearing animals also provided an important source of income to early Massachusetts pioneers. We often forget that the trappers who went West in search of the lucrative furs of the beaver, fox and bear were not only the famous explorers of the far western territories, but included many less renowned figures who broke the depths of the deep pine and deciduous forests of what we now call western and central Massachusetts.

When the Pilgrims and Puritans first settled on the Massachusetts coast, they had little idea of the immensity of the continent that lay before them. They saw an alternately rocky and sandy coast with its grasses, sedges and rushes, and the high dunes with their grassy heath, pitch pine, and scrub oak, all backed by deep forest. For the first decades of settlement they confined their explorations of Massachusetts to what geologists and geographers now consider to be one of Massachusetts' four physiographic zones: the coastal lowlands.

The coastal lowlands spread out from Narragansett Bay, cut through the middle of the state of Rhode Island, and stretch across Massachusetts to New Hampshire near the Merrimack River. The rugged shoreline, harbors and coves in many areas in the northern part of the state are evidence of ancient geological upheavals which submerged mountainous terrain. South of Boston and throughout the entire area of Cape Cod, the coastal lowland is characterized by shallow troughs and depressions eroded from softer rock. Massachusetts was entirely covered by glaciers during the last ice age, and the cape and the islands of Martha's Vineyard and Nantucket represent a

Left: *A new day begins placidly on Cape Cod.*
Facing page: *In the Berkshire hills.*
CLYDE H. SMITH PHOTOS

geological formation called a terminal moraine, a deposit of soil and rock pushed forward by the cutting edge of a glacier. The fabled rocky soil of New England—the stuff of stone fences and farmers' complaints, reputed to be the source of the Yankees' stoic character—is the debris left scattered across the land from the retreating glaciers.

A second zone is the interior lowland valley of the Connecticut and Berkshire rivers. This was originally formed from fallen land which was subsequently eroded by the rivers. Parallel to the rivers run many carved, wooded ridges formed from erosion-resistant lava from a very early volcanic age. The wide Connecticut river valley is characterized by broad and fertile meadows. It has been a rich agricultural area since the mid-18th century when it formed an important corridor linking the Massachusetts frontier and the coastal towns of Connecticut. In contrast, a second lowland valley farther to the west is the Berkshire valley, which has always been a somewhat isolated world of its own. Hemmed in by the Berkshire plateau to the east and mountain ranges to the west, it is narrow in the north, but broadens into a second fertile valley near Lenox and Great Barrington in the southwest corner of the state.

Geologists identify a third zone as the dissected uplands. There are two elevated plateaus crisscrossed by small valleys created by streams and a number of small mountain ranges. If you travel from Boston along Route 2, within a few minutes you cross a ridge, catch a last glimpse of Boston. You have just left the coastal lowlands. From there you begin a slow ascent into the first, eastern uplands, that run from Worcester to the Connecticut River. A second upland farther west is called the Berkshire hills, a continuation of the Green Mountains of Vermont. Here you will find numerous small valleys and mountain ranges with wonderful names such as Taconic and Housac. High in these ranges isolated hamlets, farms and the famous hill towns of the Berkshires such as Florida and Peru hold fast to

their independence from city ways. Found scattered throughout these uplands is the fourth distinctive geological zone of Massachusetts: the solitary remnants of once lofty mountains such as Mount Wachusett and Mount Watatic.

Each area's geography has had a strong impact on the history and the culture of Massachusetts. In the east, fishermen, clammers and sportsmen have long tapped the riches of the abundant coastal depressions, while the harbors have been home to whalers, cargo vessels and the clipper ships of the famed China Trade days. Farther inland, the falls and rapid waterways provided energy that made possible the early development of Massachusetts shoe and textile industries. The broad valleys of the Connecticut and southern Berkshire rivers have long supported truck farmers, dairies and a modest tobacco industry, while the isolated highlands of the west have preserved fascinating pockets of parochial culture which have for years been of interest to the traveler seeking a glimpse of "old" New England.

By the 18th century the true frontier had been pushed west into New York state and, as a consequence of its history of human use, there are only a few small pockets in the state of a few acres each that can be called pristine. Much of Massachusetts was cleared for agriculture centuries ago, and the forest that now covers much of the state is a second or third growth—perhaps a hundred years old or more, but certainly not the primeval wilderness that confronted the 17th-century pioneers. Most of Massachusetts is now covered with the typical northern deciduous trees: birch, beech, oaks, pine, hemlock and larch. Acres of maples put on a special show in the western part of the state each fall.

Left: On a farm near Hamilton. NANCY DUDLEY; STOCK BOSTON
Facing page: The Stockbridge Bowl in the Berkshires.
LINCOLN RUSSELL; STOCK BOSTON

Many of the familiar and beloved eastern wildflowers proliferate: white and blue violets, marsh marigold, Solomon's seal, trillium, the delicate maidenhair spleenwort and the large, graceful osmundas ferns. A common sight, especially along highways, are the extensive spreads of purple loosestrife, a wildly colorful plant ecologists spurn for the reversals its matted roots bring to wetlands.

Centuries of hunting and decades of development have greatly reduced local game and wildlife. In the mid-19th century, naturalist Louis Agassiz of Harvard University laid down the foundation for Massachusetts' subsequent preeminence in the field of natural history. Agassiz is remembered by historians of U.S. religious movements as one of the major academics in the field of natural science to unsuccessfully fight against Darwin's theory of evolution. More importantly today, he is remembered as the founder of the Marine Biological Institute at Woods Hole, long a natural history research pioneer. The Massachusetts Bureau of Fisheries, the biology and wildlife management departments in the University of Massachusetts at Amherst, the Boston Society of Natural History and the State Department of Conservation all benefited from Agassiz's work, helping to lead Massachusetts to early pre-eminence in the field.

In Boston, city fathers had the foresight to establish the Boston Park Commission in 1875. A decade later, the commission authorized the famous landscape architect Frederick Law Olmsted to ensure that Boston would be graced with trees and attractive vistas. Olmsted linked the formality of Commonwealth Avenue to the more graceful, wending gardens of the Fenway and to the large open areas of Franklin Park in

Right: The Provincetown Lighthouse on Cape Cod. BRUCE HANDS
Facing page: Near Westborough. JERRY HOWARD; STOCK BOSTON

what is often referred to as Boston's "Emerald Necklace." At about the same time, Harvard professor of horticulture Sprague Sargent converted a derelict section of Jamaica Plain into what is now the Arnold Arboretum. Another Olmsted design, the arboretum today consists of more than 120 acres of flowering trees, shrubs and plants collected from around the world.

On a state-wide scale, the Trustees of Reservations is another pioneer in protecting Massachusetts lands. Founded in 1890 to acquire scenic and historic property held in private hands, the trustees now maintain 61 sites through the state that total more than 13,600 acres of seashore, woodlands, river banks, hilltops and marshes. The organization holds conservation restrictions against building—in perpetuity—on 35 other pieces, totaling 3,870 acres. Trustee lands include the Richard T. Crane Jr. Memorial Reservation at Ipswich (a favorite beach of Boston residents), the Old Manse in Concord, the Mission House in Stockbridge and the Weir Hill Reservation in North Andover. Together with the state and federal parks and reservations, the trustees help to ensure the future of both Massachusetts land and wildlife.

As early as the 1860s Massachusetts began to respond to the adverse effects of population and industrial growth on wildlife and game species. In the 1880s the first laws regulating the hunting of game were set into effect. By the 1930s legislation had been passed for the protection of owl and hawk species. Since the 1940s, a fisheries and wildlife board composed of private citizens has played an imporant role in Massachusetts conservation by ensuring that the protection of species

Left: *Boston's parks have been part of city planning efforts for more than a century.* FRANK S. BALTHIS
Facing page: *The Arnold Aboretum.*
FREDRIK D. BODIN; STOCK BOSTON

45

would be a question of scientific management rather than political control. Today numerous government agencies, together with private organizations such as the Massachusetts Sportsmen's Council, the Massachusetts Audubon Society and the state's Nature Conservancy, work together on a variety of projects to maintain and restore Massachusetts wildlife.

Efforts have been mounted in the past several decades to restore animals that were once common features of the land. The deer herd in the commonwealth currently stands at more than 40,000 head, while the bear population, mostly in the west, has increased to between 450 and 500. After several abortive attempts to reintroduce the wild turkey back into the state in the last century, the flock has now grown to 5,000 since a successful program was started in the 1970s. Turkeys once again are hunted in the western part of the state.

The reintroduction of the Atlantic salmon is another success story for the wildlife of Massachusetts. The state's urban and industrial growth which once destroyed the Merrimack River has, over the past decade and a half spurred a grand reversal and a cleanup effort that is legendary in northeastern Massachusetts. .No one gasps when people fish the river now, and stocking programs have brought in salmon, shad, largemouth and smallmouth bass, white catfish, hornpout and carp.

Projects aimed at the restoration of the peregrine falcon and the bald eagle were established in the last decade, but it is too soon yet to know the results. A nesting pair of bald eagles, observed in central

---

Right: *The Annisquam Light, Ipswich Bay, on Massachusetts' north coast.* JAMES RANDKLEV
Facing page: *In the Parker River Wildlife Refuge near Newbury.* FREDRIK D. BODIN; STOCK BOSTON

Massachusetts' Quabbin Reservoir area in 1988, may show mating potential.

Most Massachusetts residents take for granted what people from inland states consider a luxury of the northeast: clams, lobster, oysters, scallops, shrimp and other shellfish. But the coastal zone, the ocean waters off Massachusetts and the inland wetlands are an object of particular concern to environmentalists. As a result of the booming state economy, the already densely settled state has been expanding. Recreational use and building starts on the shoreline have climbed dramatically, threatening coastal wildlife habitats. The growth of towns and cities on Cape Cod has been particularly rapid in the past decade, changing the traditionally slow-paced lifestyle of the older Cape Cod residents and further destroying cape wildlife. Harbor seals, grey seals and dolphins were once plentiful in the waters around the cape. Today, one is lucky to see them at a wildlife refuge, such as that on Monomoy Island off Chatham. Just above the cape at Plymouth, a battle is currently being waged to save the Plymouth red belly turtle, the only endangered species whose habitat is found only in Massachusetts. In the inland town of Attleboro, a fight was recently won to save local wetlands from the bulldozers of a large developer with plans for a shopping mall. One of the perennial issues hotly debated in Boston is the search for new methods of waste disposal from the growing metropolitan area and the pressing need to clean up sewage discharge into Boston harbor.

The coastal waters of Massachusetts seasonally host a variety of species of migratory whales that have in recent years become the concern of environmentalists, among them the Massachusetts branch of the

---

Left: *Fishing boats in Rockport Harbor.* JAMES RANDKLEV
Facing page: *Lobster trap buoys atop the ocean near Gloucester.*
JOHN A. LYNCH

international organization, Greenpeace. Once very plentiful, the whale populations have in more recent times dropped off drastically. Currently an estimated 2,000 humpback whales swim in the state's coastal waters. The blue whale also visits the Massachusetts shores, but in much smaller numbers. Since the 1930s the right whale has been protected but its population at present hovers at a low 300. Nevertheless whale sightings are common off the Massachusetts coast and whale watching cruises out of Boston, Plymouth and Provincetown have become popular attractions.

Massachusetts has long been known as a center for cranberry production; a native North American fruit, the tart berries were first cultivated on Cape Cod in the early 19th century. Ocean Spray now manages most of the commercial bogs in Southeastern Massachusetts and to address public interest a visitor's center has been established in Plymouth to show cultivating and harvesting methods.

A current surge of support for locally grown produce has resulted in dozens of small commercial businesses and outlets for fresh, organic produce. Massachusetts now claims eight wineries, nine farmstead cheese businesses, several sprout farms and dozens of orchards, maple sugar operations and honey producers. Hadley, Massachusetts is considered "The Asparagus Capital of the World" and come June, strawberry festivals pop up like dandelions on an unmown lawn. Country fairs such as the long established, week-long event in Topsfield still proudly judge prize-winning produce. But some secrets just don't get around. Clarence Humphrey of Woburn grew a 301-pound pumpkin a few years back, and he isn't telling anyone how he did it.

Right: *Harvesting cranberries at South Carver.*
MIRO VINTONIV; STOCK BOSTON
Facing page: *The fruits of autumn near Scituate.* JAMES RANDKLEV

CHAPTER 3

BOSTON

oston is a great tourist town. Hotels are predictably full and city sidewalks team with families wearing comfortable walking shoes. People come from all corners of the world to visit its fabulous museums, dine in its dozens of great restaurants, shop along its quaint streets. Cambridge, home of two world-famous institutions—Harvard and M.I.T.—legitimately draws a large share of visitors as the intellectual center of the area. A book that cannot be found in Harvard Square's bookstores or at the Wiedner Library probably has not been printed yet, and a staggering number of fine collections and changing exhibits from around the world keep museum-goers busy 12 months of the year.

If the natives complain about the influx, their dismay has more to do with what the visitors ask than with the space they take up. How on earth can one give directions to the Museum of Fine Arts or to Fenway Park? As out-of-town drivers soon discover, if you do not know how to get there, surely no one who knows the way can tell you in 10 words or less. It is not easy to drive in Boston if you do not know where you're going, but that's part of its charm. Much of the city's character has been very slow to change; roadways laid out for horses and carriages are not about to gracefully accommodate automobiles.

The size and shape of physical Boston has changed dramatically since its founding. When John Winthrop and the Puritans arrived in 1630 the land mass was about two miles long and one mile wide, "eaten by coves like a pear with bites in it." It sat on a peninsula with one overland access, and remained this way for 150 years. (In 1775 the British had two options for

Left: A patriotic display over Boston Harbor. CLYDE H. SMITH
Facing page: An October sunset over the Charles River paints the Boston skyline with pastels. JEFF GNASS

reaching Lexington and Concord from the foot of Boston Common—they could go "by land" over Boston Neck, now Roxbury, or "by sea" across the Charles River into Cambridge. When Paul Revere got word of their plan, he had to cross Boston Harbor to reach Charlestown, where his horse was waiting.)

In 1786 a bridge was built across the Charles River—the first of several, making Cambridge and remote towns to the west more accessible. Monumental landfill and excavation projects in the 1840s, 1850s and 1860s involved removing hills and using them, along with carted-in stone and gravel, to fill in those coves. According to Boston scholar Walter Muir Whitehill: "To visualize the limits of Boston in 1630 one must imagine away considerably more than half the land that appears on a modern map."

Boston is still largely made up of human scale architecture, in part as a result of frequent early fires which led in 1803 to a General Court law "that all buildings exceeding 10 feet high be built of stone or brick…" Some of the city's finest architecture was created by Charles Bulfinch, whose prolific career began in 1788. He built entire streets, public buildings, churches, banks, office buildings, hospitals and schools. A fine example of his extraordinary talent can be seen in the Harrison Gray Otis House, now the headquarters of the Society for the Preservation of New England Antiquities.

The lovingly preserved bowfront brick townhouses of Beacon Hill, the brick row houses of the South End, and the grand row houses of the Back Bay are best seen on foot. An easy-to-follow and informative source of

Right: *Springtime comes to Beacon Hill.*
MIKE MAZZASCHI; STOCK BOSTON
Facing page: *A quiet day on the campus of Harvard University.*
FRANK S. BALTHIS

55

specific walking tours—*Historic Walks in Old Boston* by John Harris (The Globe Pequot Press)—points out dozens of architectural landmarks and anecdotes to make them memorable.

But the Boston that's there to be enjoyed today is not a city under glass. Its historic monuments have changed along with the economy and the pulse of the city. The 5.5-mile Freedom Trail, for example, links together 16 beloved sites, many associated with the Revolution. But none of them are exactly the way they were way back when. The 50-acre Boston Common, where the trail begins, dates back to the 1630s and originally was used to graze cattle and train soldiers. (Its Frog Pond is the last survivor of several watering holes.) It was not until 1830 that Mayor Harrison Gray Otis banned cattle from the Common and city fathers first talked about a manicured park. Faneuil Hall, the famous site where orators Sam Adams and John Hancock stirred public outrage against the British is about four times as large now as it was then. And Paul Revere's House, built in 1676 and honored as Boston's oldest structure, was "fixed up" to look the way preservationists through it should; the addition Revere built for his children was removed and several improvements were made. (However, the Trail makes a fascinating, easy-to-follow journey and includes The State House, designed in 1795 by Charles Bulfinch; Park Street Church; Granary Burying Ground where Paul Revere, John Hancock, Samuel Adams and other early Bostonians rest; King's Chapel, the first Anglican church in Boston; Old South Meeting House, where participants in the Boston Tea Party were stirred into action; Old State House, built in 1713 and the first center for the colonial government;

Left: *The Old State House, Boston.* JIM CRONK
Facing page: *Old North Church, Boston, where "lo, on his sight a second lantern burned," signalling Paul Revere that British troops moved "by sea" in April 1775.* CLYDE H. SMITH

the site of the Boston Massacre; Christ Church, formerly called Old North Church, Boston's oldest church still in use, with the famous belfry where two lanterns were hung to warn Revere that the British were coming "by sea"; Bunker Hill Monument; and the U.S.S. Constitution, nicknamed Old Ironsides for her indomitable strength during the War of 1812.

Changing Power and Politics

Boston was founded by Puritans in the 17th century to be a City on a Hill that would show the world the way in which the Reformation principles of a Holy Commonwealth might be realized in the wilderness, away from the corruptions of old England. In the decades leading up to the Revolution, it became a hotbed of agitation, breeding many of the nation's early leaders, and inspiring American ideals of liberty and freedom. In the early 19th century, Boston stood at the center of the ferment of the young republic struggling to gain its sense of national identity. Whether in letters and arts or in its pioneering achievements in industrialization, Boston led the way towards the 20th century and the commonwealth, along with much of the nation, followed.

But by the end of the 19th century, Boston stood as a divided city. For the old-line Yankee brahmins, Boston was still the "Hub of the Universe," and for polite society across the nation the Back Bay and the good side of Beacon Hill remained symbols of wealth, breeding and gentility. But for the numerous immigrants and their sons and daughters, Boston became something of a war zone in which victories and defeats could be measured in the terms of cold hard cash and the struggle for political power. As if tired from its labors, Boston slipped into decline in the early decades of the 20th century.

The city temporarily renewed its strength when the Naval Shipyard in Charlestown became an important

depot during World War II, but once the mighty Massachusetts textile and shoe industries moved south after the war, its many wharves stood idle, giving in to fierce competition from the port of New York City.

In 1903, Boston was the first American city to limit the height of its buildings—70 feet near parks, 90 feet at Copley Square, 125 feet downtown. The story of three landmarks that have dominated the city's skyline at different times give an indication of Boston's fate in the first half of this century. The 25-story Custom House Tower was built in 1915 overlooking Boston's bustling port. For several decades this modest neo-classical structure towered over a low rise city of neighborhoods that had taken shape the previous century. While New York soared with the advent of the skyscraper, Boston remained loyal to its height limit in order to insure that the golden dome of the State House and the steeples of many churches remained the most prominent features of the landscape.

Then in 1947 the taller and more formidable John Hancock Building rose in the Back Bay, symbolizing that in post-war Boston the insurance and service industries would play an increasingly important role in the city's future. Boston changed at a moderate pace as the children and grandchildren of the immigrants established themselves as a part of the rising middle class.

A new spirit of growth and revival led to the construction in 1965 of Boston's first true modern office tower—the Prudential Center. Its site was formerly an extensive railroad yard that for half a century had formed a wasteland in the central city.

Left: A three-wheeled car will draw a crowd anywhere; here, at Boston's venerable Union Oyster House. FRANK H. BALTHIS
Facing page: *The skyline sparkles by night.* CLYDE H. SMITH

What is often referred to as the "New Boston" began with a political shift in 1950 when John B. Hynes, son of an Irish immigrant and a quiet career bureaucrat, was elected mayor by appealing to the new middle class. Hynes gained the support of the Irish, the Italians and the Jews, as well as the old-line Yankees, and his victory over James Michael Curley opened a new era of conciliation. John Collins, another of the new breed of Irish politician and the successor to Hynes, and his successor, another Irish American, Kevin White, continued the trend, making a new and very different Boston.

Part of the change was also an indirect result of the war. Many scientists and engineers at M.I.T. and Harvard had done wa- related work in these major universities. Choosing to call Boston home, they turned their energies to commercial enterprises and laid the foundation for what two decades later would result in Boston's "High Tech" boom. Part of the change was physical.

In the post-war years the suburbs flourished and new arteries were needed to connect the once small cities that had surrounded Boston for centuries. The result was Route 128, a new "super highway" that ringed Boston, and the Massachusetts Turnpike that linked the city to the suburbs to the west. The availability of large tracts of relatively inexpensive land and easy access combined to make Route 128 a natural home for new electronics and computer industries. A new Boston and a new metropolitan area were built from the resources in the old city: capital from the well established

Right: *Cargo-container cranes geometry, Boston Harbor.*
Facing page: *Boat rowing takes many forms on the Charles River.*
CLYDE H. SMITH PHOTOS

banking and insurance businesses; brains from the major universities; and a new better-educated generation of employees from the middle class.

With economic change, the city's skyline was not far behind. During the late 1950s and early 1960s urban renewal became a watch word in the city with often devastating consequences. An entire neighborhood— the West End—that had been home to more than 20,000 Italians and Jews for decades fell before the wrecking ball, only to be replaced with expensive high rise housing for business executives and office managers. The need for a world class airport put extraordinary pressure on another traditional neighborhood—East Boston—where entire streets were leveled for airport service roads and runways. Scollay Square, once the home of honky-tonks, burlesque and legitimate theater, was obliterated to make room for the new City Hall, an austere and inefficient building, referred to as an example of the "New Brutalism" by its critics. (A local joke describes it as looking like the box old Faneuil Hall came in.) Farther downtown, banks, insurance companies and real estate developers immortalized their accomplishments with new granite and marble-faced towers that changed the skyline overnight.

In the meantime, the population of Boston underwent corresponding changes. The middle class had begun the flight from the city in the post-war years, leaving old and dilapidated neighborhoods like the South End half-empty. The city's population dropped drastically from 800,000 in 1950 to less than 600,000 in 1970. Even stately Back Bay and the quaint streets of Beacon Hill lost their luster. The old Yankee families

Left: *The John Fitzgerald Kennedy Memorial Library, Boston.*
Facing page: *The curves, planes and cornices of different eras of architecture in the city.* CLYDE H. SMITH PHOTOS

had long since moved to fashionable communities such as Beverly and Pride's Crossing on the North Shore; rooming houses and apartments replaced the drawing rooms where the old Brahmin families had once reigned over the Hub of the Universe.

If you had come to Boston in the 1970s you would have found a city of stark contrasts. The streets of the business district, many of which had taken shape centuries before along old cow paths, were clogged with the cars of thousands of office workers commuting into the city from the suburbs. Construction was booming downtown and uptown as well, where the Christian Science Center, the sleek, mirrored John Hancock Building and the new addition to the Boston Public Library were beginning to refashion Boston's traditional landmarks. Yet at the same time, the wharves of the harbor district were literally empty and it was possible to take long, private strolls through what had once been the heart of Boston undistracted by the bustle of secretaries and executives on lunch hour just a street or two away. In the South End entire blocks of gracious brownstones and townhouses stood abandoned and the urban poor made makeshift homes amid boarded up shells.

In this decade the seeds of today's Boston sunk its roots. Thousands of students from Harvard, Tufts, Boston University, Boston College, MIT, and other local colleges and universities discovered Boston as undergraduates and decided to stay, attracted by its democratic ideals, its intellectual atmosphere, its historic aura and its tattered charm. Young professionals working in the new industries found "starter homes" in 100-year-old townhouses a subway stop away from work and turned away from tract homes in suburbs 20 or 40 miles away. For many it was a stunning revelation and a tremendous pleasure to discover that for just a few thousand dollars—and a great deal of renovation work—one could own a piece of old Boston.

The preservation of Boston's historic neighborhoods

became a top priority for many in the city. In 1955 the Massachusetts legislature created a Beacon Hill Historic District; in 1963 the entire district was designated a Registered Historic Landmark by the Department of the Interior. Similar measures to protect Back Bay, the South End, and numerous other areas and individual buildings themselves soon followed.

Renewed interest in living in the city touched off an important and controversial turn-around for the economy of Boston. Whereas one could rent a Back Bay room for $20 a week or buy a South End townhouse shell for $8,000 in 1970, a decade later prices had tripled and quadrupled, with no end in sight. What had begun as a spontaneous interest in restoring Boston's history was soon dubbed "gentrification" as the older residents of many of Boston's neighborhoods found they could not afford to coexist with the new, upscale professionals. Real estate speculation exacerbated the problem until by the 1980s the Boston area housing market had become one of the tightest, trendiest and costliest in the nation.

It is one of those ironies of history that what had begun as a period of reconciliation threatens once again to turn Boston into an ethnic and financial battleground over turf. Neighborhoods like South Boston, where for over a century the remnants of the old Irish immigrant community have retained their sense of home, or the North End, long the home for Boston's Italian community, are now threatened by speculators and condominium developers. Even Roxbury, a large black neighborhood that for half a

Left: The Massachusetts State Capitol. FRANK S. BALTHIS
Facing page: Fenway Park, home of the Boston Red Sox.
MIRO VINTONIV; STOCK BOSTON

century has been sadly neglected has now emerged as a new and potentially lucrative frontier for the next wave of urban homesteaders.

The current mayor of Boston, Ray Flynn, represents a generation of politicians who are steeped in the complex ethnic political traditions of modern Massachusetts. Flynn, the son of the Irish community of South Boston, continues to work to balance the needs of the older neighborhoods and ethnic communities with the changing face of New Boston. Of particular importance is his successful, if at times controversial, effort to link financially the highly visible and lucrative downtown development of hotels, convention halls and office towers to the less visible and attractive, but equally critical development of low-cost housing and capital improvements in the neighborhoods.

Everyone would agree that economic growth is a key element in the health and well being of the city, but protection of historic neighborhoods, both physically and socially, is also important. The route to accomplishing these goals is hotly debated. Symbols of the way in which Boston is attempting to strike compromises between the old and the new—not always successfully—abound in the streets today.

One example can be seen in the new tower recently completed at 101 Arch Street near Downtown Crossing. For more than three years the Boston Preservation Alliance waged an unsuccessful legal battle to stop the demolition of the Kennedy Department Store, an old commercial landmark, which stood on the Arch Street site. In order to strike a balance between old and new, the developer completely gutted the

Right: *Logan International Airport is one of the busiest in the United States.*
Facing page: *Symphony Hall awaits concert-goers.*
MIRO VINTONIV; STOCK BOSTON

department store, but left its brick facade standing, incorporating it into a 20-story office tower designed in what the architect has called a "Ruskin, neo-Gothic" post modern design. The reviews have been mixed. Some consider the building to be a successful solution to the problem of saving the old while making way for the new; others view it as an incredibly ugly piece of architecture.

A symbol of a different sort is found in the new Tent City development located between Back Bay and the South End. In 1968, during the heyday of Boston's traumatic demolition as a development phase, low-cost apartments that had housed 100 families were destroyed to make way for a parking lot. An interracial group of activists for the community protested by creating a tent city on the site, demanding that community housing needs be met by the Boston Redevelopment Authority, the city's planning commission. After more than a decade of protracted negotiations, a compromise solution recently came to fruition when Tent City, 269 units of mixed-income housing, recently opened its doors. Perched upon a 700-car underground parking garage, Tent City represents the kind of negotiated compromise between old and new, traditional and progressive needs, that will keep Boston both growing and liveable.

Left: *Holiday preparations near Old North Church.*
Facing page: *At work in Boston harbor.*
CLYDE H. SMITH PHOTOS

THE STATE

Massachusetts is a small state, one you can cross easily in an afternoon on the way to someplace West. But in virtually every town there are attractions to catch a visitor's eye. The traveler is advised to move slowly and allow extra time to pursue the inevitable diversions that Massachusetts offers. To provide you with a sampling of what there is to see and do, we've divided the state into six regions: Western, Central, Northeastern, Greater Boston, Southeastern, and Cape Cod and the Islands.

WESTERN MASSACHUSETTS

Attractions in the state's four western counties—Hampshire, Hampden, Franklin and Berkshire—concern history, natural beauty and the area's commitment to education and the arts. In the space of a few hours it's possible to examine dinosaur tracks, peruse a poet's personal correspondence, and pick apples or strawberries.

Literary heroes of the 19th century found inspiration in the quiet towns and pastoral scenery of the Berkshires. Herman Melville wrote *Moby Dick* in Pittsfield, where his summer home, Arrowhead, is now open to the public. The Berkshire Athenæum within the Pittsfield Public Library devotes an entire room to Melville memorabilia. Pittsfield was also the summer workplace for Oliver Wendell Holmes and Longfellow. Edith Wharton and Nathaniel Hawthorne came to Lenox. Her house, known as The Mount, and the splendid gardens she designed are open to the public, and in summer Shakespearean theater is presented at

Left: The Jug End in the Berkshire. CLYDE H. SMITH
Facing page: Heman Melville wrote Moby Dick here at the Pittsfield home he called Arrowhead. MARY ANN BROCKMAN

the outdoor amphitheater on the grounds. Hawthorne's cottage has been preserved at Tanglewood, the Boston Symphony Orchestra's 210-acre summer home. Many devoted symphony fans bring picnic suppers and stretch out on the grassy lawn to enjoy a meal with their music. A full schedule of international performers draws crowds to Jacob's Pillow in Becket, the country's oldest summer dance theater.

It was to Western Massachusetts that pioneers in higher education for women came to establish the Mount Holyoke Female Seminary (chartered as a college in 1888) in South Hadley and Smith College in Northampton, established in 1871 as the first women's college in New England. The Mount Holyoke College Art Museum displays a small, well selected collection. South Hadley is also home to C. Nash Dinosaur Land, one of several places in this part of the state where you can examine dinosaur tracks. Smith welcomes visitors all year to its Lyman Plant House and Botanical Gardens, and its Museum of Art, containing European and American paintings, sculpture, photography and prints.

Some of the country's oldest schools for men were established here, too. Amherst College, dating to 1825 and associated with the beloved American poets Emily Dickinson and Robert Frost, has two museums on campus: the Pratt Museum of Natural History, noteworthy for another collection of dinosaur footprints, specimens and American Indian exhibits, and the Mead Art Museum offering seven galleries of contemporary and classical works. The house in town

Daniel Chester French's home Chesterwood, at Stockbridge, displays copies and models of his sculptures. **Right:** *The original of this standing Lincoln graces the Nebraska capitol grounds.* **Facing page:** *Plaster casts in his studio include the seated Lincoln of the Lincoln Memorial, Washington, D.C.* MARY ANN BROCKMAN PHOTOS

where Dickinson was born and where she wrote poetry from 1855 to 1886 is open for tours by appointment, and Jones Library features an Emily Dickinson room, plus collections of her works and those of Frost. The University of Massachusetts at Amherst holds numerous events for the community at its 12-year-old Fine Arts Center, and displays an extensive collection of plants in its Durfee Conservatory.

Williamstown, a picture-perfect New England college town, is home to Williams College, which grew out of Williams Academy in 1793, and two fine art museums. On the college campus the Museum of Art contains a worldly collection, and the outstanding Sterling and Francine Clark Art Institute features an impressive number of 19th-century French paintings, English silver, prints and drawings. From June through August the Williamstown Theatre Festival stages fine productions at the college.

A site well known to old house and history lovers is Historic Deerfield, a National Historic Landmark. Its collection of 12 historic houses along a mile-long, 300 year old road treats visitors to the opportunity to actually step back in time. Its collections of American decorative arts, furniture, ceramics, glass, silver and textiles serve as valuable resources and inspiration to those interested in authentic country antiques.

The Hancock Shaker Village in Hancock, not far from Pittsfield, provides an extraordinary opportunity to gain a sense of the values shared by members of this religious sect. Restored buildings include a magnificent round stone barn, and craft demonstrations and exhibits illustrate the pure simplicity and ingenuity of the once active community.

In 1896, sculptor Daniel Chester French, creator of the Minutemen Statue in Concord and the Seated Lincoln in Washington, D.C., purchased a farm near Stockbridge, and turned it into his home and studio. Now owned by the National Trust for Historic Preservation, the site is open to the public. Visitors can see the elegant furnishings French lived with, and his well designed studio, complete with a railroad track that allowed the artist to roll his huge creations into the sunlight for close inspection.

Stockbridge itself is a popular stop on the tourist trail. The hometown of painter Norman Rockwell honors its beloved favorite son at The Norman Rockwell Museum, housing the world's largest collection of original Rockwell paintings. There are also two National Historic Sites here—Mission House, the fine 18th-century home of the Sergeant family, and Naumkeag, designed by Stanford White in 1885 as a home for Joseph Choate, U.S. Ambassador to Great Britain. Stanford White designed three other buildings in Stockbridge: a casino, now home to the Berkshire Theater Festival; the railroad station, revived as a restaurant; and St. Paul's Episcopal Church in the center of town.

Right: *University of Massachusetts, Amherst.* CLYDE H. SMITH
Facing page: *Autumn leaves carpet Deerfield.* FRANK S. BALTHIS

CENTRAL MASSACHUSETTS

Worcester County, the largest in Massachusetts, stretches the entire width of the state. In its center sits Worcester, the "heart" of the state. To escape British censorship of his radical press during the Revolution, publisher Isaiah Thomas floated his printing equipment down the Charles to Worcester, where he continued publishing his inflammatory *Massachusetts Spy*, often cited as America's first newspaper. Thomas also founded the American Antiquarian Society, faithfully dedicated to preserving printed material relating to the country's early history. A one-time industrial boom town, Worcester has recently undergone extensive restoration and revitalization, its triple-decker houses and historic homes lovingly refurbished. A bill passed in Congress in 1987 created the Blackstone Valley River National Heritage Quarter, designed to draw attention to a 46-mile corridor between Worcester and Providence considered to be the birthplace of the Industrial Revolution. Planners forsee extensive revitalization, environmental cleanup and a boost in morale for those who call this area home.

The Worcester Art Museum, with permanent collections in 33 galleries, contains outstanding collections of European, American and Oriental art, and one has only to step inside the Worcester Science Center, owned by one of the country's oldest natural history societies, to watch live polar bears swimming in icy water. The Higgins Armory Museum, with its dramatic gothic architecture, is a perfect setting for the largest display of Medieval and Renaissance armor in the country; there's even a suit of armor for a dog!

In the early 18th century restless pioneers pushed westward from Boston to clear the land and establish

Left: A misty dawn in Western Massachusetts.
STUART COHEN; STOCK BOSTON
Facing page: Looking toward the Monument Mountains from the Fountain Steps, in the Berkshires. MARY ANN BROCKMAN

communities such as Auburn, Shirley, Shrewsbury, Fitchburg and Athol, all of which proudly have preserved their historic houses and mementoes from those early days.

Sturbridge Village in Sturbridge, one of the Northeast's most popular attractions, presents visitors with a recreated 1830s rural community and a chance to wander through a Massachusetts town of years ago. Occupying 200 acres, with a working farm, costumed interpreters and hands-on demonstrations of the way things used to be done, the village sponsors year-round special events. Reservations for its traditional Thanksgiving Day meals must be made *years* in advance. Benefiting from the steady stream of visitors to town, Sturbridge is also home to the Fairbanks Doll Museum, boasting at least one of every doll ever manufactured in America, and the Sturbridge Auto Museum, displaying vintage steam, gas and electric cars from 1897 to 1939. Brimfield, not far from Sturbridge, hosts extensive, town-wide flea markets in May, July and September. Growing out of a family tradition and now covering acres of dealers plus dozens of yard sales lining Route 20, the colossal events run from Thursday through Sunday.

Between 1835 and 1845 a number of Utopian experiments sprouted up in Massachusetts. One of the most radical was Fruitlands, created in Harvard by Bronson Alcott and his English friend Charles Lane, who urged members of their "consociate family" to form spiritual ties and forgo the pleasures of sex, tobacco, alcohol and meat. Visitors can tour the farmhouse where Alcott dreamed of escaping "a world lost in materialism," and on the grounds tour small museums devoted to Shaker crafts, American Indian artifacts and art exhibits.

Webster, so named in the mid-19th century to honor statesman Daniel Webster, is home to a lexical

Left and facing page: History lives at Sturbridge Village.
BRUCE HANDS

landmark: the longest place name in the United States goes to the local lake, which the Indians called Chargoggagoggmanchauggagoggchaubunagungamaugg. Loosely interpreted, it means: "You fish on your side of the lake, I'll fish on mine, and no one will fish in the middle." Locals call it Webster Lake and use it for boating and water skiing.

Quabbin Reservoir, man-made in the 1940s at the expense of Enfield, which now lies below it, is a prized spot for picnics and bird watching. In 1982 four fledgling bald eagles were released here, and today, chances of seeing a living representative of our national symbol are excellent. (Quabbin Tower atop the highest point in Quabbin Park, Enfield Lookout, and Goodnough Dike are three good spots for sighting eagles.)

Central Massachusetts is home to several small, specialized museums that are well worth a detour: Willard House & Clock Museum in Grafton commemorates the 18th-century birthplace of the famed Willard clocks and displays a fine collection; American Optical Museum, honoring a 150-year old local industry, exhibits an extensive collection of antique eyeglass frames and related items in Southbridge; Fisher Museum of Forestry in Petersham, run by the Harvard University Forestry Department, contains dioramas and offers fine trails for hiking; Lancaster's Military Museum at Fort Devens owns memorabilia dating to the Revolution; and Toy Cupboard Puppet Theatre and Museum in Oxford offers a good collection of early marionettes and stages seasonal puppet shows. Oxford has honored Clara Barton, founder of the American Red Cross, by preserving her family homestead and furnishings.

Right: *Staff and visitors at Sturbridge Village.*
STUART COHEN; STOCK BOSTON
Facing page: *What would autumn be without Indian corn?*
BRUCE BERG

NORTHEAST MASSACHUSETTS

Several decades before the Pilgrims landed at Plymouth, Englishmen fished the seas and established temporary settlements for salting codfish along Massachusetts' "other cape," Cape Ann. In 1623 a contingent of Puritans from Dorchester established a fishing station in what is now Gloucester and in the 1700s more fishing fleets sailed from this port than any other in New England. In the center of town, the Fishermen's Memorial, a bronze sailor sculpted by Leonard Craske, looks out to sea and stands as a lasting reminder of the generations of hard-working men who never returned home from the sea. For a less somber sense of the town, visit Beauport Museum, a 26-room showplace furnished with American and European decorative arts by avant garde interior designer Henry Sleeper.

Other charming North Shore seaside towns still contain a goodly share of summer homes and people who can afford to frequent them. They have also become beloved haunts for day trippers from Boston. Manchester is famous for its lovely Singing Beach, so named for the sound its sand makes when walked upon. Ipswich, which borders both the Ipswich River and the ocean, provides another spot popular with Boston sun seekers at Crane Beach, just below Castle Hill, the estate built in the 1920s by Richard Crane of plumbing fixture fame. The John Whipple House on Ipswich's Main Street dates to 1640 and is one of the oldest houses left standing in the country. When you stand before its huge fireplaces you immediately feel its builder's determination to outwit the New England winters.

Left: *Dinghies in Smith Cove on Rocky Neck, Gloucester.*
Facing page: *The historic Blackburn Inn in Gloucester.*
BRUCE HANDS PHOTOS

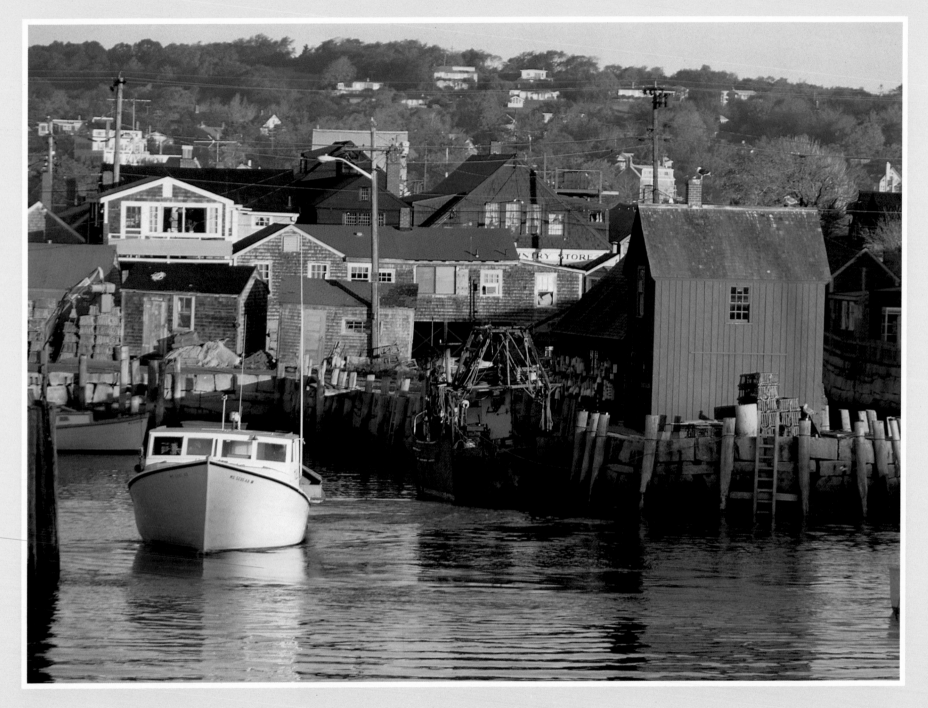

Rockport, once a sleepy fishing village, is known to artists as the location of a red fishing shed, fondly called Motif Number One, one of the most painted and photographed scenes in America. (When a severe storm destroyed the shed, it was quickly restored right on the site.) The paper house here, made entirely of newspapers, is an architectural oddity worth seeking out.

Marblehead, settled in 1629 by seasoned fishermen from Cornwall and the Channel Islands, is close enough to serve as a bedroom community for Boston commuters. It retains a salty charm throughout the streets of Old Town, where several former homes of sea captains have been preserved for public visits. From Crocker Park one can look out on the harbor, a sailor's paradise that is virtually filled with boats. The Victorian red brick Abbott Hall which dominates the town contains the largest known version of Willard's famous patriotic painting, *The Spirit of '76*.

The U.S. Coast Guard was founded in Newburyport in 1790, a once thriving shipbuilding center and fishing port. A devastating fire leveled the town in the early 1800s and it was rebuilt, serving today as a fine example of Federalist seaside architecture. Both state and federal funds have helped Newburyport gain new life as a renovated and now bustling tourist town with good restaurants and well stocked shops. Fowles Drugstore in the center of town has resisted change and remains a 1940s Art Moderne treasure with its black carrara glass storefront, 1930s neon sign, wooden booths and streamlined steel grill and soda fountain. In nearby Newbury, the Plum Island National Wildlife Refuge

Right: *The traditional symbol of welcome, the pineapple, on a Marblehead home.* BRUCE HANDS
Facing page: *Rockport.* ROBERT PERRON

offers terrific birding and a splendid, unspoiled stretch of ocean beach.

For a brief period in the early 19th century Salem was the busiest seaport in America. Dozens of well preserved sea captains' mansions make this another architectural wonderland to explore on foot. Chestnut Street, laid out in 1796, is lined with Federal masterpieces, most notably those built by native son Samuel McIntire. Essex Institute, a complex of several historic homes, displays fine furnishings typically found in the Salem of 200 years ago. The Peabody Museum, the oldest continuously operating museum in the United States, is rich in Massachusetts maritime memorabilia. (The fine collection from the former Museum of the American China Trade in Milton is now owned by the Peabody.) Nine waterfront acres that figured prominently into 19th-century Salem—including a custom house, warehouse, store, wharf and several historic houses— have been designated the Salem Maritime Historic Site. Salem still garners plenty of attention as "Witch City," although the infamous witch trials of the late 17th century actually took place in Salem Village, which changed its name to Danvers in 1757. Tourists are lured into the Salem Witch Museum, where 13 stage sets recreate the trials, and the Witch Dungeon Museum, which stages live reenactments. The most famous of Salem's landmarks is The House of Seven Gables, said to have inspired Nathaniel Hawthorne's novel concerning the effects of witchcraft.

Beverly, known for the magnificent estates of Beverly Farms, Pride's Crossing and Montserrat, contains more

Left: *The House of the Seven Gables, at Salem.* JIM CRONK
Facing page: *Good Harbor Beach, Gloucester.* BRUCE HANDS

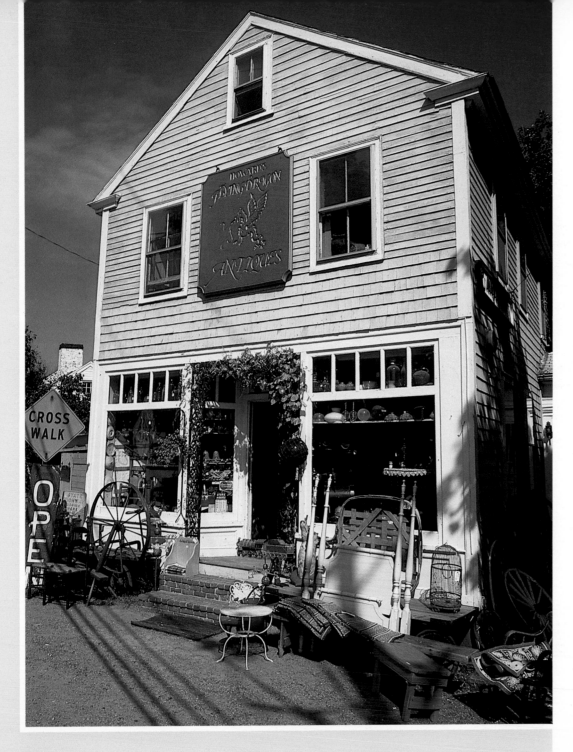

fine examples of early New England architecture, most notably Balch House, built in 1636 and one of the oldest wooden frame houses in the United States. In summer and fall, Hamilton's exclusive Myopia Polo Club opens its doors to the public for Sunday afternoon polo matches and in Wenham, one of New England's oldest tea houses offers afternoon refreshments in a quaint setting.

Northeastern Massachusetts is also rich in sites relating to the Industrial Revolution. The oldest is the Saugus Iron Works National Historic Site, complete with a recreated 17th-century iron works and blast furnace, rolling mill and ironworker's house. In North Andover, the Museum of the American Textile History displays exhibits relating to American textile history and hosts a wonderfully entertaining annual Sheep Shearing Festival in May.

The state-wide Massachusetts Urban Heritage State Park program, designed to restore important mill architecture and revitalize former eyesores with green spaces, esplanades and parks, now gives three industrial cities in this section of the state a healthy piece of the tourism pie. In Lowell, a textile center built upon plans mentally smuggled out of England by Francis Cabot Lowell in 1810, close to six miles of canals have been cleaned up for barge tours, and a multi-image slide show tells the story of the city's development. In Lawrence, a city carved out of Merrimack River hillsides in the 1840s that produced up to 800 miles of cloth a day, a worker's boarding house has been restored as a visitor's center and extensive landscaped paths radiate from a

Left: Antiquing in Massachusetts (here, at Essex) is a passion for many residents, as well as tourists. BRUCE HANDS

Facing page: Only 24 years later, Massachusetts honored those who fell by "the rude bridge that arched the flood" and shed the first patriot blood of the American Revolution. JIM CRONK

fountain dedicated to Robert Frost, a beloved native son. And in Lynn, once a major shoemaking center, the Lynn Heritage State Park offers walkways along the harbor and features a reconstructed cobbler's shop in its visitors center.

The Northeast has had its share of famous residents, among them poet and abolitionist John Greenleaf Whittier, whose home in Amesbury is open to the public. Mary Baker Eddy, founder of the Christian Science Church, also lived in Amesbury and Swampscott; both of her houses now welcome visitors. On the campus of the prestigious Andover Academy the Addison Gallery of American Art displays a fine collection of ship models and works from the 18th century to the present.

GREATER BOSTON

In March of 1775, Revolutionary agitators Sam Adams and John Hancock moved several hours away from Boston to escape the watchful eye of British General Gage and to be in close contact with the countrymen who formed the militia. Their hideaway was in Lexington, a town that today is considered an easy fifteen minute commute to Boston. Superhighways radiating out from "The Hub" to the North, West and South unite a web of suburban communities, including Lexington, that are tied to Boston for employment, nightlife and cultural attractions, but that have their own long histories and retain their own separate identities. Each offers special attractions and sites that are popular with residents and visitors alike. West of Boston, it is easy to cross unknowingly into Brookline until one encounters street after leafy street of spacious homes. On May 29, 1917, John F. Kennedy was born at 83 Beals Street, a house that is now a National Historic Site. The Brookline home and office of Frederick Law Olmsted, who landscaped vast stretches of Boston and New York, has also been designated a National Historic Site. In Waltham, America's first non-sectarian Jewish-

founded university—Brandeis University—accepted its first students in 1948. On the campus overlooking the Charles River, the Rose Art Museum displays changing exhibits in five galleries. The stately Lyman House, built by Samuel McIntire in 1793, still has several of its early greenhouses and is a popular spot for gardeners.

Watertown was selected as the site for a U.S. arsenal in 1816 and, starting with the Civil War, guns and ammunition were made here. The extensive complex still stands, but now fuels the war of inflation; it has become a shopping mall. In 1912, the Perkins School for the Blind came to Watertown and gained a solid reputation for its students Helen Keller and her teacher, Annie Sullivan.

Wellesley is a college town. Here Wellesley College was founded in 1875 and Babson College in 1919. On Wellesley's campus the Jewett Arts Center displays changing shows and the Margaret Ferguson Greenhouses put on seasonal displays; Babson's Coleman Map Building contains the world's largest relief map of the United States—65 feet long, 45 feet wide. The view of it from the balcony simulates a vantage point of 700 miles above the earth. An enormous 28-foot globe behind the building weighs 25 tons.

Weston was designated in 1988 as the most expensive suburb in America in which to buy a house. Its splendid Case Estates, owned by Boston's Arnold Arboretum, features 110 acres of natural woodland and cultivated plantings. On the campus of Regis College the Cardinal Spellman Philatelic Museum attracts scholars of world-wide postal history and stamps. Its

Left: *In the Eleanor Elkins Rice Memorial Library at Harvard.*
Facing page: *Name your pastime at outdoor tables in Cambridge.*
FRANK S. BALTHIS

collection includes more than 300,000 stamps and its museum store contains great gift ideas for philatelists.

Lexington and Concord are perhaps the most visited towns in Massachusetts. Every April 19 the Revolutionary War battles that propelled America into outright war with England are reenacted by troops in period dress, and thousands of visitors pay homage on this day and throughout the year, starting with the Lexington Green and its statue of Captain John Parker, brave captain of the Lexington militia. Buckman Tavern, across the street, where the militiamen assembled that morning, is open for tours, as is the Hancock-Clarke House, where Sam Adams and John Hancock were warned by Paul Revere of the British approach. Concord's famous day is commemorated by the Minuteman National Historic Park on Liberty Street. Its reconstructed North Bridge, scene of "the shot heard round the world," is set off by Daniel Chester French's defiant minuteman statue.

In the 19th century Concord attracted a host of Massachusetts intellectuals including Emerson, Hawthorne, the Alcotts and Thoreau, who went to the woods, built a cabin, and wrote about the experience in *Walden*. Walden Pond, a popular swimming spot in summer, has been preserved as a state reservation, and a replica of Thoreau's cabin can be seen at the Thoreau Lyceum, also in Concord. The contents of Emerson's study are on display at the Concord Antiquarian Museum, and the homes where Hawthorne, Emerson and the Alcotts lived are also open as museums.

Right: *Emerson's home in Concord.* ROBERT PERRON
Facing page: *The Old North Bridge in Concord, where redcoats fired "the shot heard 'round the world" on April 19, 1775.*
JIM CRONK

To the South of Boston lies Dedham, where Jonathan Fairbanks built a wooden frame house in 1636 that is still standing, rivaling Beverly's claim to the oldest house in America. In 1921 the eyes of the world focused on this suburban community when the Sacco and Vanzetti trial took place at the Norfolk County Courthouse.

SOUTHEAST

Commuters who live on the South Shore curse "The Expressway"—Route 3— their only link to Boston and the road traveled by people heading to and from Cape Cod. The tradeoff for battling the traffic is that they can live in lovely towns such as Hingham, Duxbury, Cohasset and Norwell.

Close by Boston, the expressway cuts through Quincy, first settled in 1625 by the notorious Captain Wollaston and Thomas Morton, who turned their backs on Puritanism and among other festivities had the audacity to celebrate spring with drink, a May Pole and dancing. Today Quincy is rich in Adams family lore: four generations of Adamses, including second and sixth presidents John and John Quincy, lived in the house that has been designated the Adams National Historic Site. The birthplaces of both presidents are also open to the public.

Hingham, settled in 1632, is one of the oldest communities in Massachusetts. Its magnificent Old Ship Church, so named because its massive beams come together in the shape of an inverted ship's hull, holds steadfastly to its claim as the oldest church in the United States to remain in continuous service; a fire in

Left: The Mayflower replica at Plymouth.
PETER SOUTHWICK; STOCK BOSTON
Facing page: At the Adams National Historic Site, Quincy.
JIM CRONK

the winter of 1987 damaged some nearby structures, but spared the old church.

Plymouth and Bristol counties have been central to the early history and industrial development of Massachusetts. The Pilgrims and their first Thanksgiving are imbedded in our souls and a visit to Plymouth demands confronting the legend up close: there's Plymouth Rock; a replica of the *Mayflower* that carried those 102 men, women and children across the ocean in 1620; Plimoth Plantation, a village recreated to have the look and feel of the first Pilgrim colony; and Pilgrim Hall Museum, where items once owned by the Pilgrims are on display.

In the early 19th century New Bedford eclipsed Nantucket as the state's major whaling port, and by 1850 more than 650 of its whalers cruised both the Altantic and the Pacific. The city is a good place to wander in search of memories from those long ago days. The Whaling Museum features an outstanding collection of scrimshaw—objects whittled from whalebone and delicately etched by sailors passing the time on their long sea voyages. The museum owns one of America's longest paintings—Benjamin Russell's *Panorama of a Whaling Voyage Around the World*—in total measuring 1,375 feet long and showing a voyage which crossed all seven seas. Across the street from the museum, the Seaman's Bethel, founded in 1830 to save seamen's souls, honors the pew Heman Melville chose when he lived in town. One of New Bedford's strongest images is the Whaleman Statue in the public library yard, dedicated to the whaler's motto: "A dead whale or a stove boat."

Right: *Plimouth Plantation provides 20th-century eyes a view of life in the 17th century.* CARY WOLINSKI; STOCK BOSTON
Facing page: *New Bedford, one-time whaling capital.*
CLYDE H. SMITH

New Bedford's port location made it a natural site for industrial development and the New Bedford Glass Museum recalls the early Pairpont and Mount Washington glass companies here. Along with nearby Fall River, the city became a major textile center in the mid-19th century. The visitor center at the Fall River Heritage State Park features changing exhibits on the area's industrial development.

Fall River was once the place to catch a steamship to Newport or New York. Although transportation visionaries still talk about reviving boat links between Massachusetts and New York, the closest you can come to those glory days of overnight cruises is the Marine Museum's fine collection of ship models and memorabilia concerning the grand days of steam travel. Commemorating another kind of ocean voyage, Battleship Cove recalls navy life on the sea during World War II. The U.S.S. *Massachusetts*, the U.S.S. *Joseph P. Kennedy Jr.*, PT Boat 796 and the submarine *Lionfish* are all open for public inspection.

It was in Fall River that Lizzie Borden was tried and acquitted of the ax murders of her father and stepmother on August 4, 1892. The crime so captivated the country that decades later it still figures into our national folklore, inspiring rhymes such as "Lizzie Borden took an ax and gave her father 40 whacks…" That ax, by the way, is displayed along with other Lizzie items, at the Fall River Historical Society.

Architecture enthusiasts make pilgrimages to Easton, an industrial town during the Civil War, which features several fine examples of Henry Hobson Richardson's work. These include the Oliver Ames Free Public

Left: Sunrise at Westport Point. NONA BAUER
Facing page: Saltwater taffy goes with seashores; here, at Provincetown. FRANK S. BALTHIS

Library (its carvings and gargoyles were created by Richardson's friend, Stanford White, and its bronze mantle bas relief was sculpted by Augustus St. Gaudens), Ames Memorial Hall (landscaped by Frederick Law Olmsted), the railroad station, the Ames Gate House (private), and the Gardner's Cottage (also private). A few miles east is Brockton, whose once busy shoe industry kept the Union army shod during the Civil War. The Brockton Art Center within the 700-acre Field Park presents an active calendar of special shows.

CAPE COD AND THE ISLANDS

Cape Cod and the islands of Nantucket and Martha's Vineyard are nobody's secret, and getting to them on summer weekends demands more than a sightseer's interest. Those with strong constitutions (the planes are small) and reservations can get avoid the traffic snarls by flying from Boston to Hyannis, Provincetown, or either island.

Over the past few decades the cape has become a year-round community for a large segment of the state's senior citizens who have winterized summer cottages and built new homes. The second home market was booming in the 1970s and dozens of communities that once dozed through the winter woke up too late to stop the residential sprawl. Natives lament the outrageous prices of homes, worry about the water supply, curse the season-long traffic jams, and watch the service industries suffer—no one can afford to live here on a busboy's or supermarket clerk's salary.

But the hundreds of miles of ocean frontage, and moderate climate do make this part of Massachusetts irresistible, especially in the off-season when the crowds are gone. It takes but a minute to inherit an awesome respect for the Cape Cod National Seashore, spearheaded by President Kennedy, which protects from development 40 miles of ocean beach and thousands of acres of land from Eastham to Provincetown. Visitor's

centers for the Seashore in Eastham and Provincetown provide excellent information on plant and animal life, along with maps of hiking trails and bike paths.

Daytrippers will board a boat in Boston and step off it three hours later in Provincetown, on the very tip of Cape Cod. Visited by Myles Standish and other Puritan explorers in the 17th century, the port became a solid Portuguese fishing community. Its charming cottages, winding streets and sense of being at land's end attracted an impressive colony of artists in the early decades of this century. The carefree winds of the 1960s blew through Provincetown, causing patrons of the Chrysler Art Museum to move their fine collection to the South and fueling fears that the town was doomed. Today, Provincetown flourishes as a tourist town and a gay and lesbian community, offering good food, trendy shops and galleries. The climb to the top of the Pilgrim Monument is worth the effort for the spectacular view.

To explore the natural beauty of the cape set aside time to visit Monomoy National Wildlife Refuge, accessible by boat from Chatham; the Ashumet Holly Reservation in Falmouth and the Welfleet Bay Wildlife Sanctuary in Wellfleet, both maintained by the Massachusetts Audubon Society. Local sea life is displayed in Woods Hole at the National Marine Fisheries Aquarium, and the New Alchemy Institute in East Falmouth shares its inspirational success with solar greenhouses, aquaculture and organic gardening.

Nantucket, included as part of the Plymouth Colony in 1621, first attracted independent settlers who turned to whaling for their livelihood. It remained a busy whaling port until 1820. The Whaling Museum displays an interesting collection of items relating to the long sea voyages and hard work of chasing and capturing whales, and will acquaint visitors with the awesome size of a hand-thrown harpoon. The town's cobblestone streets and delightful architecture make it an ideal spot for walking. In the 1970s its harborfront was "revitalized," much to the dismay of those who preferred its weathered charm. The Jared Coffin House, a charming and historic old inn on the island, charges $100 and up per night for a double room and is booked up well in advance. Many locals have converted every available spare room into bed and breakfast lodging that can be had for more reasonable prices.

Martha's Vineyard, the larger and closer of the two islands, remains a summer retreat for the rich and famous. Vineyard Haven, up island, is accessible by auto ferry from Woods Hole or by passenger ferry from Falmouth, Hyannis, or New Bedford. It is the island's commercial center, its good harbor protected by the outcroppings of West Chop and East Chop.

One of the most photographed and beloved towns on the Vineyard is Oak Bluffs, which began as a Methodist meeting camp and grew into a colony of Victorian homes with elaborately carved gingerbread trim. The Flying Horses carousel here, with its authentic carved wooden horses, is said to be the oldest still operating in the country.

Right: *Vineyard Haven on Martha's Vineyard.* CLYDE H. SMITH
Facing page: *The Nobska Light at Woods Hole.* JOHN A. LYNCH

For Further Reading

The Berkshire Book. Jonathan Sternfield. Berkshire House, Great Barrington, 1981.

A Book for Boston. David R. Godine, Boston, 1980.

Boston: City on a Hill. Andrew Buni and Alan Rogers. Windsor Publications, Woodland Hills, Calif., 1984.

Boston: A Topographical History. Walter Muir Whitehill. Belknap Press, Cambridge, Mass., 1968.

The Commemorative Guide to the Massachusetts Bicentennial, edited by Georgia Orcutt. Yankee Inc., Dublin, NH, 1975.

Historic Walks in Old Boston. John Harris. The Globe Pequot Press, Chester, Conn., 1982.

Massachusetts. Federal Writer's Project. Houghton Mifflin, Boston, 1937.

Massachusetts: From the Berkshires to the Cape. Walter Muir Whitehill. Viking Press, New York, 1977.

Yankee Superlatives. Georgia Orcutt, ed. Yankee Inc., Dublin, NH, 1977.

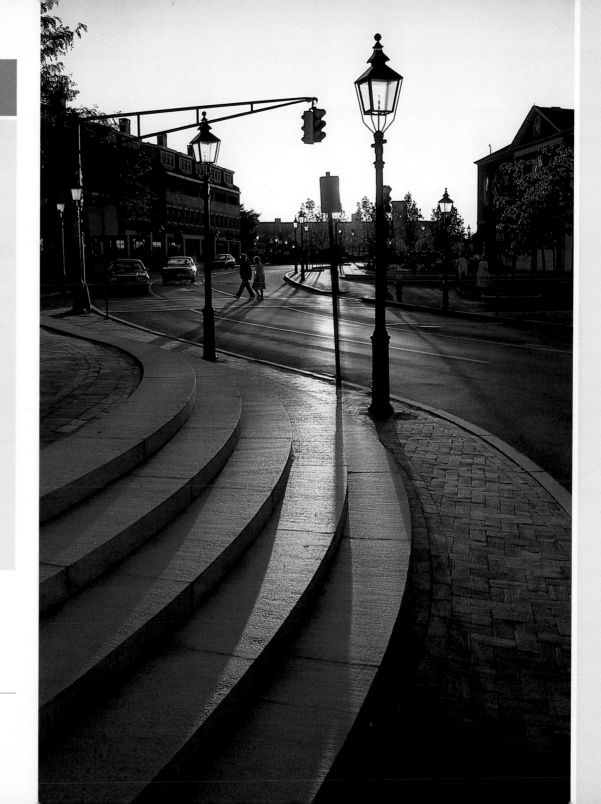

Right: *Newburyport's Market Square at sunset.* BRUCE HANDS
Facing page: *Night lights in Nantucket.* CLYDE H. SMITH

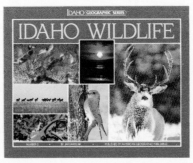

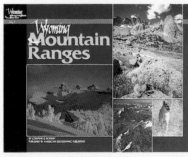

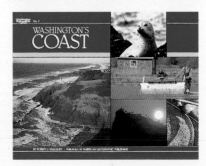